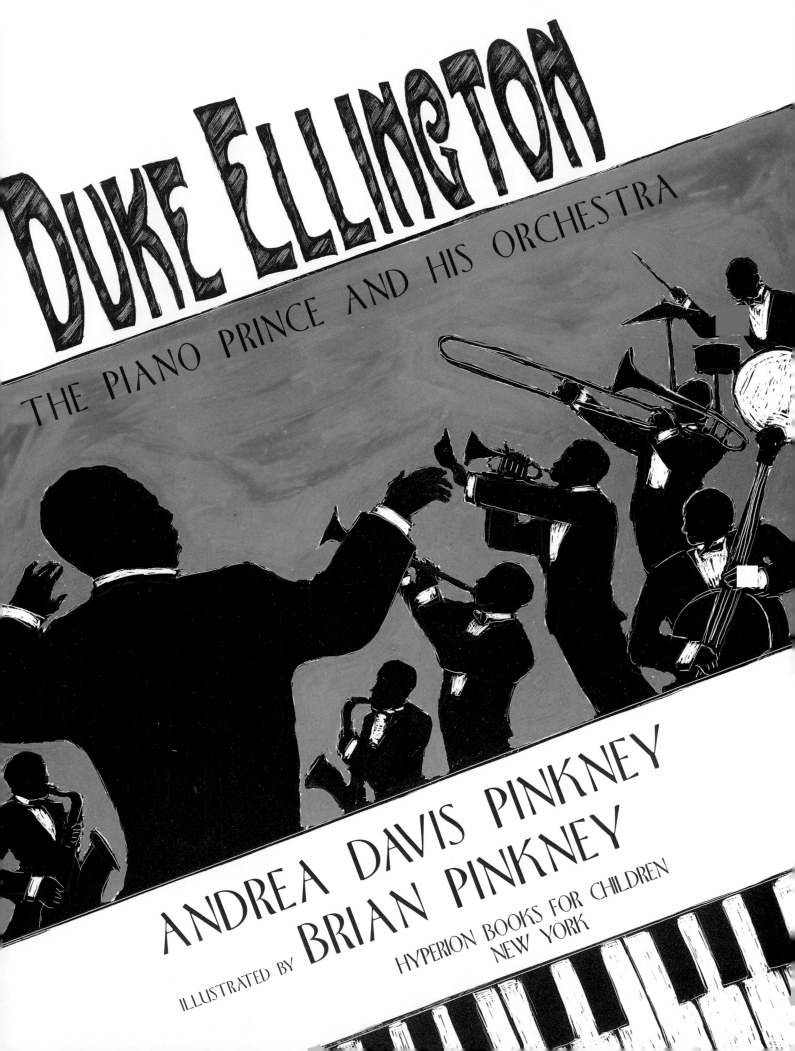

DUKE ELLINGTON

THE PIANO PRINCE AND HIS ORCHESTRA

ANDREA DAVIS PINKNEY

ILLUSTRATED BY BRIAN PINKNEY

HYPERION BOOKS FOR CHILDREN
NEW YORK

You ever hear of the jazz-playin' man, the man with the cats who could swing with his band? He was born in 1899, in Washington, D.C. Born Edward Kennedy Ellington. But wherever young Edward went, he said, "Hey, call me Duke."

Duke's name fit him rightly. He was a smooth-talkin', slick-steppin', piano-playin' kid. But his piano playing wasn't always as breezy as his stride. When Duke's mother, Daisy, and his father, J. E., enrolled him in piano lessons, Duke didn't want to go. Baseball was Duke's idea of fun. But his parents had other notions for their child.

Duke had to start with the piano basics, his fingers playing the same tired tune—*one-and-two-and-one-and-two*. Daisy and J. E. made Duke practice day after day.

To Duke, *one-and-two* wasn't music. He called it an *umpy-dump* sound that was headed nowhere worth following. He quit his lessons and kissed the piano a fast good-bye.

Years later, on a steamy summer night, Duke heard that *umpy-dump* played in a whole new way. Folks called the music ragtime—piano that turned *umpy-dump* into a soul-rousing romp.

The ragtime music set Duke's fingers to wiggling. Soon he was back at the piano, trying to plunk out his own ragtime rhythm. *One-and-two-and-one-and-two* . . . At first, this was the only crude tinkling Duke knew.

But with practice, all Duke's fingers rode the piano keys. Duke started to play his own made-up melodies. Whole notes, chords, sharps, and flats. Left-handed hops and right-handed slides.

Believe it, man. Duke taught himself to press on the pearlies like nobody else could. His *one-and-two-umpy-dump* became a thing of the past. Now, playing the piano was Duke's all-time love.

When Duke was nineteen, he was entertaining ladies and gents at parties, pool halls, country clubs, and cabarets. He had fine-as-pie good looks and flashy threads. He was a ladies' man, with flair to spare. And whenever a pretty-skinned beauty leaned on Duke's piano, he played his best music, compositions smoother than a hairdo sleeked with pomade.

It wasn't long before Duke formed his own small band, a group of musicians who played all over Washington, D.C. But soon they split the D.C. scene and made tracks for New York City—for Harlem, the place where jazz music ruled.

They called themselves the Washingtonians, and performed in all kinds of New York City honky-tonks. Barron's Exclusive. The Plantation. Ciro's. And the Kentucky Club. Folks got to know the band by name and came to hear them play.

Then, on an autumn day in 1927, Lady Luck smiled pretty on the Washingtonians. They were asked to play at the Cotton Club, Harlem's swankiest hangout, a big-time nightspot.

The Cotton Club became a regular gig for Duke and his band. They grew to twelve musicians and changed their name to Duke Ellington and His Orchestra. Night after night, they played their music, which was broadcast live over the radio.

F or all those homebodies out in radio-lovers'
land—folks who only dreamed of sitting pretty at
the Cotton—the show helped them feel like they were
out on the town. Duke's *Creole Love Call* was spicier than a pot of
jambalaya. His *Mood Indigo* was a musical stream that swelled over the
airwaves.

ometimes the Orchestra performed their tunes straight-up. But
other nights, when the joint started to jump, Duke told his band
to play whatever came to mind—to improvise their solos. To
make the music fly! And they did.

Each instrument raised its own voice. One by one, each cat took
the floor and wiped it clean with his own special way of
playing. Sonny Greer pounded out the bang of jump-rope
feet on the street with his snare drum. A subway beat
on his bass drum. A sassy ride on his cymbal.
Sonny's percussion was smooth and steady.
Sometimes only his drumsticks made the
music, cracking out the rattly beat of
wood slapping wood.

Along with Sonny, Joe "Tricky Sam" Nanton went to work on his trombone, sliding smooth melodic gold. He stretched the notes to their full tilt, pushing and pulling their tropical lilt. When Tricky Sam was through, he'd nod to Otto "Toby" Hardwick. "Your turn," he'd say. "Take the floor, Daddy-O!"

Toby let loose on his sleek brass sax, curling his notes like a kite tail in the wind. A musical loop-de-loop, with a serious twist.

Last came James "Bubber" Miley, a one-of-a-kind horn player. He could make his trumpet wail like a man whose blues were deeper than the deep blue sea. To stir up the sound of his low-moan horn, Bubber turned out a growl from way down in his throat. His gutbucket tunes put a spell on the room.

Yeah,
those solos
were kickin'. Hot-buttered
bop, with lots of sassy-cool tones.
When the band did their thing, the Cotton Club
performers danced the Black Bottom, the Fish-Tail, and the Suzy-Q.
And while they were cuttin' the rug, Duke slid his honey-colored
fingertips across the ivory eighty-eights.

The word on Duke and his band spread, from New York to Macon to Kalamazoo and on to the sunshiny Hollywood Hills. The whole country soon swung to Duke's beat. Once folks got a taste of Duke's soul-sweet music, they hurried to the record stores, asking:

"Yo, you got the Duke?"

"Slide me some King of the Keys, please!"

"Gonna play me that Piano Prince and his band!"

People bought Duke's records—thousands of them.

In 1939, Duke hired Billy Strayhorn, a musician who wrote songs. Billy became Duke's ace, his main man. Duke and Billy worked as a team. Together they composed unforgettable music. Billy's song *Take the "A" Train* was one of the greatest hits of 1941.

With the tunes that he and Billy wrote,
Duke painted colors with his band's sound. He
could swirl the butterscotch tones of Tricky Sam's horn with the silver
notes of the alto saxophones. And, ooh, those clarinets. Duke could blend
their red-hot blips with a purple dash of brass from the trumpet section.

In time, folks said Duke Ellington's *real* instrument wasn't his piano at
all—it was his Orchestra. Most people called his music jazz. But Duke
called it "the music of my people."

And to celebrate the history of African-American people, Duke composed a special suite he called *Black, Brown, and Beige*. A suite that rocked
the bosom and lifted the soul.

Black, Brown, and Beige sang the glories of dark skin, the pride of
African heritage, and the triumphs of black people, from the days of
slavery to years of civil rights struggle.

Duke introduced *Black, Brown, and Beige* at New York's Carnegie Hall, a symphony hall so grand that even the seats wore velvet. Few African-Americans had played at Carnegie Hall before. Duke and his Orchestra performed on January 23, 1943. Outside, the winter wind was cold and slapping. But inside, Carnegie Hall was sizzling with applause. Duke had become a master maestro.

Because of Duke's genius, his Orchestra now had a musical mix like no other.

Now you've heard of the jazz-playin' man. The man with the cats who could swing with his band.

King of the Keys.

Piano Prince.

Edward Kennedy Ellington.

The Duke.

Truly a Duke

Edward Kennedy "Duke" Ellington, born April 29, 1899, was a forerunner in the evolution of jazz. He composed and played swing music, one of the best-loved jazz forms to grace the American music scene.

The roots of jazz encompass several types of music—blues, ragtime, folk music, and marches—that originated from the musical traditions of African-American people. Since its birth in the early twentieth century, jazz has grown to include many styles that remain popular today.

In 1927 Duke Ellington and His Orchestra began a highly successful engagement at Harlem's renowned Cotton Club, a run that lasted five years. By the early 1930s Duke began to produce complex, original arrangements that resembled the music of classical orchestras, yet were still popular among all kinds of music lovers. *Sophisticated Lady* and *I Got It Bad* are among the most memorable.

Duke composed some of these tunes together with Billy Strayhorn, which made his band a force to be reckoned with. Duke's Orchestra toured the United States and abroad, delighting audiences wherever they went.

On January 23, 1943, Duke performed a concert at Carnegie Hall. Though some jazz musicians had played there before, few had performed elaborate music like Duke's. Duke wrote *Black, Brown, and Beige* especially for the event. This composition showed the world that Duke Ellington was an accomplished composer, a symphonic master whose music had come to be regarded as beyond category.

During the more than fifty years of his celebrated career, Duke wrote and composed at least one thousand compositions (some say as many as five thousand), including ballet and film scores, orchestral suites, musicals, and choral works. More

than eight hundred musicians appeared with his Orchestra during its years on the road.

Duke Ellington died on May 24, 1974, but his musical genius is far from gone. His influence on the history of music—and on musicians every-where—continues even today.

Sources

Bibliography

Blum, Stella, ed. *Everyday Fashions of the Twenties*. New York: Dover Publications, 1981.

Boyd, Bill, arr. *Music of Duke Ellington*. Milwaukee, Wis.: Hal Leonard Corporation, 1995.

Collier, James Lincoln. *Duke Ellington*. New York: Collier Books, Macmillan Publishing Co., 1991.

Driggs, Frank, and Harris Lewine. *Black Beauty, White Heat: A Pictorial History of Classic Jazz, 1920–1950*. New York: Da Capo Press, 1995.

Edey, Maitland A., ed. *This Fabulous Century, vols. 1–4*. New York: Time-Life Books, 1969.

Ellington, Duke. *Music Is My Mistress*. New York: Doubleday, 1973.

Frankl, Ron. *Duke Ellington*. New York: Chelsea House Publishers, 1988.

Haskins, James. *Black Dance in America*. New York: HarperCollins Publishers, 1990.

Haskins, Jim. *The Cotton Club*. New York: New American Library, 1977.

Kaplin, Margaret L., and Charles Miers, eds. *Harlem Renaissance—Art of Black America*. New York: The Studio Museum in Harlem/Harry N. Abrams, 1987.

Monceaux, Morgan. *Jazz: My Music, My People*. New York: Alfred A. Knopf, 1994.

Schoener, Allon, ed. *Harlem on My Mind: Cultural Capital of Black America 1900–1968*. New York: Random House, 1968.

Videography

Jazz Classics—Duke Ellington and His Orchestra 1929–1941. Rahway, N.J.: Amvest Video, 1987.

Jazz Classics—Harlem Harmonies, vol. I. 1940–1945. Rahway, N.J.: Videofidelity, 1986.

Jazz Classics—Harlem Harmonies, vol. II. 1941–1946. Rahway, N.J.: Amvest Video, 1987.

Museum Exhibitions

"Beyond Category: The Musical Genius of Duke Ellington." The Museum of the City of New York, New York, October 9, 1993–March 29, 1994.

For Chloe Grace, who fills us with music
—A. D. P. & B. P.

Acknowledgments:
Special thanks to Carnegie Hall Archives and the Museum of the City of New York for their research assistance.

The text for this book is set in 16-point Cochin. The artwork for each picture is prepared as scratchboard renderings with luma dyes, gouache, and oil paint.

Printed in Singapore.

FIRST EDITION
1 3 5 7 9 10 8 6 4 2

Library of Congress Cataloging-in-Publication Data
Pinkney, Andrea Davis.
Duke Ellington / Andrea Davis Pinkney ; illustrated by Brian Pinkney—1st ed.
p.   cm.
Includes bibliography references.
Summary: A brief recounting of the career of this jazz musician and composer, who, along with his orchestra, created music that was beyond category.
ISBN 0-7868-0178-6 (trade)—ISBN 0-7868-2150-7 (lib. bdg.)
1. Ellington, Duke, 1899–1974—Juvenile literature.   2. Jazz musicians—United States—Biography—Juvenile literature.
[1. Ellington, Duke, 1899–1974.   2. Musicians.   3. Afro-Americans—Biography.]
I. Pinkney, J. Brian, ill.   II. Title.
ML3930.E44P56   1997
781.65'092—dc20   [B]   96-46031